# Traveling Through

*Selected Poems by*

# Eveline Landau Kanes

*Finishing Line Press*
Georgetown, Kentucky

# Traveling Through

## ACKNOWLEDGMENTS

Previously published:

"Spindlermuhle, 1930s," "Fever Remedies," "Old Photographs," "Lives Laid
Bare," "Nine Years," appeared in *A Coin Worn Thin*, Finishing Line Press, 2015.

"Kandinsky," appeared in *Voices Israel,* Poetry from Israel and Abroad, Vol.35,
2009.

"Autumn Thoughts," appeared in *White Pelican Review*, Vol X, Nr. 2, Fall, 2009.

"Freud's Sofa," appeared in *The Common Ground Review*, Fall/Winter Stars
Issue, Vol. 2, 2016.

I want to thank Leah Maines and Christen Kincaid for their unfailing support.

I am also exceedingly grateful to Judit Muller and Robert Kanes for the cover
design and photos.

Thanks, also, to Marylee McNeal, for all her helpful suggestions.

Publisher: Leah Maines
Editor: Christen Kincaid
Cover Art: Robert Kanes
Author Photo: Robert Kanes
Cover Design: Judy Muller

Order online: www.finishinglinepress.com
        also available on amazon.com

Author inquiries and mail orders:
Finishing Line Press
P. O. Box 1626
Georgetown, Kentucky 40324
U. S. A.

# Table of Contents

*For My Family*

*Traveling Through My Life*
*I have traveled many miles*
*crossed two continents*
*each stage a landmark*

# Family Memories

# Spindlermuhle, 1930s

So clear that night
        and still,
only the sound
        of the horse's hooves
on packed snow
        and the sleigh bells
broke the silence,
        our breaths mingled
with the horse's steam
        as we huddled under
a heavy blanket
        my parents and I
alert to the brightness
        of moon-lit sky
so young, so long ago.

## Fever Remedies

My mother treated my fevers
     with heat
she stoked me with hot lemonade, and aspirin,
     I grew to hate the pill's
innocent whiteness
     nothing disguised
its bitter taste.
     Featherbed, blankets
induced fearful dreams,
     wild dogs with fiery eyes
chased me through
     a gamut of sicknesses
as I endured hellish heat
     and Grimm dreams.

# To My Father


Most European professionals
        practiced in their homes
as did my father,
        a dental surgeon.
When our apartment bell rang
        I used to peek
into the waiting room
        to see who was there.
I knew some of them,
        ladies who always smiled
and praised my blond braids.
One day five years old
        I snuck
into the surgery and hid
        in the back of the closet
where my father's white
        coats hung.
It was very dark in there
        and no one would see me.
The closet door
        never closed properly
and through a crack
        I could watch my father.
After a very long time
I saw a lady spit blood
        into the cuspidor.
It was too much for me,
        feeling dizzy
I tunbled out
        shocking doctor and patient.
My irate father excused
        himself
carried me into my room
        put me on the bed
and forbade me to move
        until my mother called me.
I felt chastened but daring.

## Aunt Frieda

Frieda overflowed
       each chair she sat in
a black silk dress
       billowing around her,
an ample lap for an ugly
       small black dog
who eyed me suspiciously
       when Frieda guided
my four-year-old hand
       across his bristly fur.
We did not like each other,
       when Frieda put him down
he yipped at me
       and padded royally ahead
as I crept behind him
       waiting for my chance
to yank his short stub
       imitation of a tail.
He turned and snarled
       and I outran him
back to that ample lap
       for comfort and forgiveness,
she stroked my head
       and popped a chocolate
into my eager mouth.

# Old Photographs, 1930's

There I sit age seven
  posed on a river's rock
picture-perfect
  in a *Dirndl*
an *Alpenstock*
  across my knees.
There I stand age nine
  posing in an English arbor
framed by wisteria
  right foot forward
as if about to dance.
It's 1939 the camera
  has caught a carefree
summer's light before
  our world turned dark.

## Lives Laid Bare

Lives laid bare
      in documents
are skeletal lives
      without description,
no young or old
      only date of birth
presumed date of death,
      nothing to presage
incomplete lives
      cut short by bureaucrats
who dealt only in numbers,
      so much human life
total value nothing.

# Nine Years

*For Dorinda*


School children's voices
        an affirmation of life
from the other side
        of the fence
as I stand here with you
        dear Dorinda
not for the first time
        in all the nine years
since you left us.
Your daughter
        takes the old flowers
from their holder as I arrange
        a new splash of color
for the bare stone.
In the silence
        broken by happy voices
I become again
        a small German girl
whom you welcomed
        to her new home
in her own language.
Your comforting presence
        gave me hope then
and over the years
you were my sister
        whom I still mourn.

# Your Father

*For My Husband*

Such a thin thread
        held you to him
but did not break.
When his tea steamed
        on the uncle's table
and the horsehair sofa
        scratched your bare legs
you toasted him with
        your grape juice.
Cigar smoke swirled
        as you waited, bored
listening to the clock
        wheezing along
so slowly you thought
        its chime told
of a different time.
You thought you knew
        your father who dreamt
of a farm as he walked
        hoping a city's miles could
turn into a pile of coins
        at the end of each day.
You did not know
that for all unspoken words
        he held his love in the hand
that stroked your head.

# Test for a Junior Lifeguard

*For Robert*

Far in the distance
          a small head bobs
more buoy than boy
churning through waves
          daunting us on the beach.
We watch our son
          fight his way back
until triumphant
          he beaches himself
a hero gasping for air.

# Early Creations

*For Richard*


Four years old
    at school in France
your valiant
    small hand's
cursive *Maman*
    stumbled off
its intended
    printed line.
Later
    with more control
stick figures
    morphed
into painted
    lead soldiers
each one a knight
    proudly displaying
his special emblem.

# Looking and Listening

# Rhythm

It governs our lives
        not just the heart's
steady beat
        that sometimes
accelerates
        but continues to turn
each year's corner.

Rhythm thrums
        as rain on the sill
hums in the alarm clock's
        insistent voice
in the metronomic tock
        of our days
bouncing against each other.

# Beckett and Giacometti

*A Photograph, 1961*


They stand in the artist's studio
       both looking up at what we must
assume is there, sharing a kinship
       of absolute abstraction,
Beckett who seeks beyond each word
       Giacometti believer in reduction,
each is concerned with paring down
       to bone of man, unspoken word.

# Kandinsky

When he subdues the urge
       to bisect so precisely
and to contain all
       in a cocoon of gray
or black and white
       then our eyes follow
all the colored dots
       and wisps willing
any shape to be a sun
       any curve
to fly.

## Schubert's Maidens

There comes a dark stranger
        astride a black horse
he scours the landscape
        scooping up maidens
as they sit by streams
        or lean over bridges
as they gather bouquets
        or walk in the woods.
These maidens are languid
        they pine for their millers
shepherds and wanderers
        until held by the stranger.
They swoon and move
        to the black horse's rhythm
unaware they ride into a void.

# Edvard Munch—The Kiss

*Oil Painting, 1897*

Far from the gentle sinuous
      embrace of Rodin's "Kiss"
this only hints at a man's
      hulking form and face
more predator than eager lover
      as he engulfs a shapeless other.
They stand inside a murky room
      lit only from the street outside
a vision of a threatening Eros
      Munch does not want to hide.

## Matisse as Sculptor

He freed himself
          from older masters
sculpting as if wielding
          a brush shaping sinuous
tactile heads or torsos
          and velvety odalisques.
His final work in bronze
          four massive figures
in relief their backs to us
          Oceanic in their sturdiness.

# Transfigured Night

Transfigured night, its silence
       shimmers calm and luminous,
Schoenberg entranced, touched
       by the moon's caressing fingers
hears an unbroken harmony of light
       gentle at first then swelling
fading and welling up again,
       in ecstasy he claims the night

# Mahler

*Vale* Mahler sings
to an empire puffing
whiffs of decadence,
an empire become
a limping old man,
no grandiose blares
of trumpets can boost
his funereal march.
*Vale* Mahler sings
*Vale* echo the crows.

# A Gift

*For my Husband*

Wrenched by
a bitter-sweet feeling
      you watch and listen
      as other fingers play
your violin,
      old friend companion
since your childhood.
This young musician
      strives to bring out
your instrument's
      warm tones to please
your anxious ear,
      unites with you
softens your loss.

# Playing Dominoes in Prison

*A Gordon Parks Photograph*


A grainy light falls
        from a single window
onto a grid of cells.
        Dark faces in shadow
yet one man's arms
        dangle outside the bars
at rest between moves.
        His game reflects
our larger world
        where black and white
should also be aligned.

# Dismantling Rameses' Temple

Dwarfed by the grandeur
      of the Temple's scale
a ghostly legion stands
      and gapes in disbelief.
A mammoth witness
      of their toil and pain
is being dissected
      into giant slabs
to move on to another
      place and rise again.
It is a modern miracle,
      Rameses' giant head
so gently hoisted
      by a crane.

# A Concert at Mills College, California

Old and new blend in this hall
where cello soars and percussion
        challenges our ears
where the eye moves from
        modern murals
to walls with lettered
        medieval manuscripts
reminders of Gregorian melodies
        of monks who believed in the soul released
once flesh is reduced
        to bare bones.
*Anima mea* and Hallelujah
        to that which survives us.

# Ai Wei Wei Visits a Migrant Camp

Only you who also knew
      hunger and loss of freedom
could walk in the tracks
      of those who had to leave
carrying their nomansland
      inside them.
Only you could gather
      muddy blankets sweaters
a lone shoe and detritus
      left behind.
Only you could serve
      as witness
you who cleaned
      all you chose for exhibit
to restore human dignity.

# The Journey Continues

# April

April, when Nature
        throws off
her winter blanket
        wakes all her creatures
bids them call out
        to find a mate.
April, birthday month
        of the Bard who trains
our ears to listen
        for the music in each word
we choose to write.
April, not the cruelest month
        for on its first day
we jest and tease
        and laugh at each other

# Freud's Sofa, London

Now a museum piece
       this musty old sofa
holds secrets and confessions,
many a solid citizen
       has lain there weeping
in anger or relief,
all seeking a father
       more benign than their own.
Conservators have cleaned
       and mended the linen cover
fixed recalcitrant springs,
       and with each puff of dust
an aged sigh is released
       to drift into guilt-free space.

# Pierrot

*For Jean-Louis Barrault*

Pierrot came to my house
       danced for me
twirled slowly
       as we watched
moon-streaked water,
       no child of paradise I
yet he kissed me lightly
       and pirouetted
out the door.

# Provence

*Paysage de Van Gogh*
      with its mauve fields
of lavender its yellow
      undulating waves of wheat
and always the sunflowers
      those *tourne-sols* turning
their yearning faces
      toward a fickle sun.
Dark green cypress
      stand like lean sentinels or
signposts from another time,
      it is the light, *lumière,*
that informs everything.

# Wharenui = A Maori Meeting House

*New Zealand, 2006*

Eyes, eyes
      shell eyes everywhere
eyes that see all
      and forewarn,
masks with bared teeth
      to frighten wild beasts
and enemies,
      whirls of color
for a swirling world
      in which its people ask
for peace and plenty.

# Argentina's Dark Period

*1970-1980*


Matched and unmatched
      these boots and shoes
remain for bereaved
      wives or mothers
relics of the disappeared.
No sign of battle here
      no bodies, only those
leather tokens that bear
      witness to invisible feet
marching under the earth.

# Shadows in Gaza

Shadows in a shattered landscape
      picking through the shards
of their broken lives,
      who can hear a donkey bray
or the cicada tolling the hours,
      faint on the breeze the *muezzin's*
call, absent the scent
      of citrus and olive, buried
among slabs of cement
      a *finjan* gleams
its copper skin answers the sun.

# In the Month of May

It snowed in New Orleans
        in the month of May,
a warm wind lifted a fine
        sifted powdery snow
from freshly baked *beignets*
        coating everyone,
wafting onto the tables
        where black-clad bikers sat
dripping onto their beards
        printing swirls on their shirts.
In the background musicians
        welcomed the morning
as our sprinkled feet
        tapped to their rhythm.

# Street Song, Bowery N.Y.


Lost, lost
      bewildered stare
anguished eyes
      in crumpled face
mouth silent
      tongue forgetting
how to shape sounds.
      Always the same route
pushing his life
      ahead of him.

## For Stanley Kunitz

Old Lamplighter,
        your friends call you magician,
as each bright circle sparks
        they feel the touch of your wand.
Old charmer of snakes,
        their heads sway to the tune
of your silent lips,
        they shed their skins at your feet.

# An East Coast Porch, Albany 1, N.Y.

Splashes of red
        autumn's first signals
flash through this gray day.
        Even the hobbled movements
of squirrels seem more urgent
        they sense the season's
quick leap forward.
In the mornings
        our local politician
still stands on his porch.
        When he stretches and points
his cigar at the park
        he exhales unkept promises.

# Autumn Thoughts, Albany 2, N.Y.

Our dog has winter
        in his bones
and the same hand
        that set the trees alight
and burnished pumpkins
        on grey porches
now guides him
        in his last attempt
to let his memory loose
        among the rotting leaves.
Above, a black
        jumble of birds
straggles across the sky
        until a sudden signal
breaks up the tangle
        and forms the arrow
of their flight.

# Staten Island Ferry

Round-eyed perplexed
  a small girl stares
at the man who buffs
  to the ferry's rhythm,
Incredulous that he should
  kneel before another man
fixed on the mirror surface
  of the shoes before him
which will reflect nothing
  not even the discomfort
of the man who stands tall.

## Oceans

We share a long
        history yet our eyes
cannot guess their size
        beyond the horizon.
We fear the roiling waves
        when tempests push
them ashore preferring
        a gentler lapping touch,
yet in the end
        even the tides
take our castles away.

# California

*For Yves Bonnefoy*

"How vast it is," a French poet
      said looking at our landscape,
indeed for him whose inner eye
      has created subtler scenes
our natural grandeur stretching
      from hills to ocean is unmatched.

How we delight in our
      Northern self which grabs
fistfuls of mist from the ocean
      to shroud the night then lifts
that white veil for a morning sky
      whose blue spills over the water.

Our special Northen light
      favors dry hump-backed hills
in summer painting them gold
      until evening when shadows
add a purple tinge for one
      unique moment
before turning them dark,
      a constant gift.

# Asilomar Beach, California

Silence, omnipresent, timeless
      unbroken even by the surf
advancing at a steady pace
      its riders soundless too.
We walk with the bay to our left,
      dunes on the right are covered
in such clumps of sparse scrub
      as can survive winds and sea air.
I want to hold on to this silence
      cling to each wave, each dune,
even the mist-laden sky.
Back home I find pebbles,
      memoir of our walk inscribed
on the soles of my shoes.

# San Juan Bautista Evening, California

A ripe fig sunset stains the sky
      before it turns a deeper shade
as darkness drifts in the arcade
      cooling its stones, settling
behind the shuttered glass.
      Faint light is filtered through
one broken slat where we can
      glimpse a still life of two men
at cards, quite unaware of us
      as we fade back into the dusk.

# View from Crissy Field, San Francisco

Our favorite hills
  have painted
their brown coats
  with specks of green.
Our favorite bridge
  is pushing
its shoulders upward
  from a hazy mist
determined to emerge
  before the day is done.
Even a short walk
  can still fill us
with a sense
  of wonder.

# Stock Car Racing, California

*A Photograph*

It's all there:
      dirt from the track
ingrained in vibrant
      hues, painted yellow 4P
naming the owner
      of this car.

Unseen but sensed
      the sweating pit crew
as they hustle,
      their stained hands
ready for last minute
      fine-tuning.
Even the car's snarl
      joining the roar
of its competitors
      is there, a disdainful
belch of exhaust
      wafting into the night.

# Evening, San Francisco

Silence unspools on our street
        winds itself around each house
to soften sounds as the last
        of the traffic's exhaled fumes
disperses over the rooftops.
Even the mockingbird has ceased
        its repetitive song to find sleep,
only the leathery magnolia leaves
        scraping along the pavement
break the calm spell
        as time holds its breath.

# California Tragedy

Where are the gentler winds
        of older poetry
Zephyrs, were they not?
Not ours, that fan
        the fiery sparks
into a fury in their wake
        leaving all homeless
all seeking shelter.
Trees are bowed down
        their arms broken
by dangling wires,
        cars have become
melted pools,
grape vines are crushed
        impotent to withstand
the onslaught.
A brief respite
        before rain rushes
down now denuded hills
        and forms a tsunami of mud
engulfing all in its path.
Entire houses are uprooted
        owners search in the rubble.
An urn has landed
        on its side
ashes dispersed.
In these battles
there are no winners.

## Shadow Puppet

At night
       he climbs down
from the frame
       I hear him tapping
on the floor
       unused to moving
without his puppeteer.
He moves slowly
       sniffs in corners
brushes aside
       scurrying spiders
looks up in wonder
       at the photographs
on our walls.
In Indonesia
       he told
his stories
       to villagers,
men and women
       separated
by a white sheet.
All would sit
       in awe cowed
by his dark face
       and beard
his jeweled neck
       and arms
his fancy robe.
When ensconced
       in a frame
he misses
       his audience.

# Sisyphus

He did not roll
      his gigantic ball gladly
conscious each day
      of the Ancients'
absurd punishment,
      knowing he would never
reach the mountain top.
What might he have found
      had he arrived at his goal?
What do we find as we roll
      our lives before us each day,
when empty sheets of paper
      whirl past us and we try
to catch each drifting word?

## An Orphan Egg

I found it,
      a perfect small egg
abandoned by its mother
      on our deck
where it lay ruffled
      by the cold morning air.
I held it,
      cradling it in my hands
knowing their warmth
      could not replace a mother
who should have enfolded
      and cared for it to birth.

# A Storm

A howling wolf of a wind
      lashes at trees forcing eucalyptus
to their knees breaking off limbs,
      he does not merely howl at the moon
across whose bleary face he whips
      each wadded mass of clouds
until they shed their extra weight
      to share relief with a parched earth.
This wolf can slice off roofs as if
      in play and push the swollen rivers
to make waterways in streets.
      After the havoc nature's voice
intones she still controls the earth.

# Our Mourning Doves

Our mourning doves have
        come and gone
brief tenants this year
        under the deck.
Later we saw
        one small white egg
inside the fragile nest
        on which the parents
sat in turn.
Such a short stay
no sign of carnage
        only one tiny feather
signaled the occupants
        departed in haste.

# Our Tree

I always forget
       its botanical name
but I watch
       the leaves rustling
as the trunk
       tells them stories
garnered over
       its lifetime.
They listen intently
       like all children
who love stories.

# Disagreeing with Nietzsche

Let's not abandon memory
      we should recall each day
to tell our years apart
      though Nietzsche said:
without forgetting
      it is impossible
to live at all.

# Cave Art

Everything slips into silence
        and a symbolic loneliness
awaits our modern eyes
        to read the animals
poised in their flight
        on these dark walls
painted by men who
        needed to reach out
and ask some unknown
        higher being for good
hunting without strife.

# Eclipse

A lemon sliver of a moon
       its icy fingers seeking warmth
advances slowly on the sun
       whose eyelids start to droop
in unexpected lassitude
       overcome by blackness
denser than the grayest
       drifting clouds.
Once moon and sun
       have become one
time's hands push moon
       to its accustomed place.

# Language

When Roman Senators
        addressed the Senate
their sentences crafted
        from years of study
they spoke to history
        intending their words
to survive them;
        they did not speak
to arouse the populace
        unless bread and circuses
were called for.
        Now that words
our politicians speak
        have so polluted language
we must choose
        with infinite care
what passes
        across our tongues.

## Our Remarkable Times

Words now elastic
       and contorted
into invented shapes.
Democracy, Ethics,
       Honor, strong words
being stretched
       beyond recognition.

# Our Homeless

Their lives contained
        in carts and backpacks
they walk determined
        each day a destination
no walls or obligations.
Their voices often raised
        they cluster and debate
weather food shelter
        needing to move on
in an endless march.

# Bees, September 2017

Swirling in a wild
        Fandango
among a plum tree's
        white blossoms,
confused by pollen
        in September
they twirl
        and circulate.
A meringue cloud
        hovers above the tree
observing
        the dancing bees.
Did they find pollen
        again next Spring?

# Tears

Our moon
        is impartial
as it looks down
        on all
in our land,
        it silvers
everyone's tears
        and gently
strokes them away.

## Two Sisters

In the still night
      on the wind's breeze
Liberty calls out
      to her sister Justice,
"Stand tall sister
      with your scales
held high
      as do I
with my torch,"
      and in unison
the sisters say
      "all are equal,
welcome to all."

# Time

Time is snapping at my heels
      yawping louder these days,
it follows me everywhere
      and brooks no leash
as it stalks my progress.
What song can I sing
      to drown its bark
and slow its pursuit,
      go at my own pace?
Dreamlines, songlines,
      time still on a walkabout
across my face,
      in the mirror I see its tracks.

Eveline L. Kanes' Chap Book, *A Coin Worn Thin* was published in 2015, Finishing Line Press.

As a translator of German poetry her work appeared in *Alembic, Beacons, Chicago Review, Denver Quarterly, Exquisite Corpse, Grove, International Poetry Review, Modern Poetry in Translation, New Orleans Review, Poet Lore, The German Library (Gottfried Ben Anthology), Translation,* and *Visions.*

In 1994 she received a grant from the Witter Bynner Poetry Foundation for her collection *My Country Language: Ten Romanian Poets,* which was published by the Romanian Cultural Foundation in 1999.

Her other book translations range from biography and fiction to history and sociology.

www.ingramcontent.com/pod-product-compliance
Lightning Source LLC
Chambersburg PA
CBHW021158090426
42740CB00008B/1140